SIMPLY JSCRIPT

Getting Started on the Right foot

Richard Thomas Edwards

INTRODUCTION

Two guys walk into a local bar. Both just got told they were no longer needed at their last place of business.

"See they got you, too," says one observing the usual signs of disappointment.

"Yep", he confesses. "Not needed down at the mailroom."

"Me, too", says the other.

The bartender plucks down a square napkin and pours both a large glass of scotch.

"Looks like the two of you are down on your luck. This one is on the house."

"I'd take anything just to make ends meet," Says the first guy.

"Anything," asks the bartender. " I've got a job for a bar back. Pays $12 bucks and hour."

"I'll take it!", says the first guy.

"What are you going to do," asks the bartender. Pointing his stare towards the second fellow.

"Me?", begins the second guy. "I'm going to do something radical. I'm going to land a job in IT."

Well, two years later, the bar back becomes the bartender and he's making $15 per hour $50 per night tips. So he's pulling in around $4000 clear per month.

In comes the guy he met two years later wearing geeky looking clothes like he's on vacation and sits down at the bar.

"I know you," begins the bartender. "You were the guy I met here two years ago."

"Yes," admits the second guy, "I was. And I see you've moved up from bar back to bartender. Congratulations."

"Thank you," says the bartender acting smug. So, what's your story?"

"Me?", the other guy began, well I left here that night and decided I was going to break the chains of mediocrity, paid my rent and gave notice. I moved to Tucson, AZ. I got a job there and devoted the rest of my time to learning programming."

"Okay, and then what happened," asks bartender.

"Ever heard of Silly App?" he asks.

The bartender shrugged his shoulders, "Sure, who hasn't. It's one of the most popular apps on a cell phones."

"Well, I wrote it. Here's my card. Give me a holler if you or someone else who comes in here one night not looking a job but looking for a new way to do something that is really big besides the daily 9 to 5 grind. I'm heading out tonight for a well-deserved vacation."

The bartender couldn't help but notice the limo pulling up out in front of the bar.

And as the man walked out of the bar, he looked at the business card. Simple in its design, it said:

> Steven Smith
> Adventure Group Inc, LLC
> President and CEO
> "Come join us if you want to change the world"

"Well, I guess he did," said the bartender.

The point to this story should be pretty clear. One man was given the opportunity to work right away and took it. The other wanted to change the world, reduced his costs and learned how to program smart phones. He then had an idea for a smart phone application and made millions.

That is the power of programming.

CONTENTS

Working with The Right Stuff

It is all about you having the skills you need

This morning it arrived. It came to me because a man who wants to make money needed to communicate with me over the Internet that he had something I wanted, knew where to get it and made it incredibly easy for me to get.

It was a book entitled: **MIND YOUR OWN BUSINESS;** and was edited by Stephen Wagner & the Editors of Income Opportunities Magazine.

I was one of those Editors. And I wanted as a reference to my accomplishments over the years. There were two articles of mine in it. It is part of my constantly growing legacy and an example of how I enjoy sharing what I know with others.

Someone wrote a program for the man who wanted to make money. In fact, more than one someone wrote programs to get me that book.

All I did was perform a search and put in the right keywords. What do you know, there it was.

One of those someone's could have been you. And if it was, thank you for you for your time, effort and talents. For certain, you've made my day.

If you are not one of those people who made my day and are one of many people reading this wishing you could become something bigger than life, or wanting to learn how to code, you are definitely on track for doing so.

I don't pretend that this is going to be an easy road for you. Nothing worthwhile is.

What I do know is the quicker you jump in with both feet, the faster it will be for you to get the point where you can start looking for work from what you have learned.

How can I make such a promise?

Because I have been where you are today. and I know how hard it is to get to where I am today and I want to make it a lot easier for you to accomplish the same dream.

Which brings us to motives. Without them, there's no reason to want to learn.

1. You want to learn a new language for your own personal reasons
2. You want to teach a new language to others.
3. You want a job and you think VBScript is the best way to get one.
4. You have a job and was asked to do something in code to accomplish a task.
5. You have a not going anywhere job and learning a language is your salvation.
6. You love working with your computer and want to know more about what it does
7. You don't start yelling at the technical support people when they ask you to do something.
8. You own or rent Office 365 and you want to customize it to suit your needs.
9. You already know VBScript but would like to understand more so you can improve on your skills.
10. You hate having stuff on your computer when you have no idea what it does. (And are afraid to find out.)
11. You want the computer to do more than collect dust when you are at work.
12. You like to learn through trial and error.

Okay, so here's what I expect from you. In order to get the most out of this book, you will need the following:

1. A computer that works
2. Know how to type – I'll take the old two finger typing at this point
3. Know how to use the mouse
4. Know how to get to things on your computer – like the menu.
5. Know what a command prompt is
6. Be willing to type lines on the command line and see what it does
7. Have some sort version of Microsoft Office installed
8. Be willing to install trial software such as SQL Server.
9. Be willing to install Visual Studio 2017 Community Edition
10. Be willing to spend at least an hour a day learning a new language
11. Be willing to learn how to read code
12. Be willing to do a lot of cutting and pasting

If you are willing and able to do all of the above, then we have a statement of work the two of us can share.

Programming is a Job

I t's a job. A 9 to 5 grind. Often thankless, taken for granted and I dare say these days being terribly under paid for the services rendered.

Never-the-less, it is a job you can do and – I might add – do it much smarter and faster. Who cares what they are paying when you can get the job done 3 times faster than they thought and you can spend the rest of the learning what you need to know to take it to the next level and pay raise.

After all, what I'm about to tell you is going to line up your tactical offense so profoundly that if you were a football team, you're be going to the Super Bowl.

Listen, programming is truly amazing!

It is also a lot of hard work.

Back in my day Duke Nukem, Jane Of The Jungle and Wolfenstein 3D suddenly became more interesting than learning how to become a programmer. Had I given in, I would have not gone to work for Microsoft 1 year later.

The interesting thing about it, at the time I was teaching myself how to program in VB3, Microsoft wasn't on my radar.

What was, on my radar was surviving in the back of a store in Maple Shade, New Jersey with a mean junk yard dog Rottweiler by the name of Bruno. Whom which he and I became good friends. So much so that one day when customer leaned too far over the counter where I was working, Bruno when unglued. No one got hurt. But that was a far cry from day one when I thought he was going to bite my head off.

Kind of like learning code. Not knowing can eat your lunch, learning can become a bread earner.

And then there was this job.

WHO THE HECK IS WORLDNET
Another boring but true story

This is a totally true story and one that should go down in the annuals of life changing events.

After returning from my Maple Shade, New Jersey efforts of learning VB3, I met up with a young man by the name of Dennis who own Del-Tech Computers In Lake Charles, LA.

Dennis and his father, who owned The Thrifty Nickel, decided that purchasing a franchise of an Internet provider. The only problem in 1995, was there was no installer program and so, he made a deal with me that if I could create a installer program for it, he would let me use a copy of VB4 Professional to do it with.

Well, through a couple of months of trial and error, the installer program for Windows 95 was created and tested.

Now, Dennis wanted this program to work on Windows 311 for workgroups. I was so new to programming, I had no idea why the program wouldn't work on that OS. After all, it is Windows, isn't it?

Anyway, I got a call from International Maintenance Corporation to go on a job as a Millwright at GSU – getting paid $17\hour back then was much more important to me than a program I was speculating on something that I didn't understand why it wasn't working on 3.11 for workgroups– and so, I took the job. Well, that rolled right into a turnaround at CIGTO Refinery and that didn't end until April.

I felt pretty bad about leaving Dennis's working half way done. So, as soon as the turnaround was over, I talked with Dennis as he was about to go out the door and asked him if he and the company were still interested. He said yes and then I asked him "what would be the worse-case scenario", and he told me, "Well, the worse-case scenario would be I would have a hell of a work experience to add to my resume."

That statement perplexed me. The floppy I was holding had a black ball with lines in it going horizontal and vertical and had the letters WorldNet on it.

Who the heck was WorldNet?

It wasn't until I got to Seattle in July and was watching TV that I learned it was AT&T WorldNet.

It's amazing what a $90 support call back in Lake Charles, LA would have done to help me understand the fact that the only thing I needed was to install Window 311 for workgroups and the 16-bit version of VB4 needed to be installed on it. After that, the copying the code over to it would have completed the job.

In the beginning

n the beginning, there was Assembly, C, C++ and then JAVA came around and all hell broke loose. Finally, when the time was right, JavaScript was introduced to the coffee Internet community and programmers spent tons of money learning it.

Then Microsoft came along and decided .

They said, you know what, we can create our own version of JavaScript and we will call it JScript.

Well, JScript programmers started scratching their heads. They couldn't understand why Microsoft thought re-inventing the wheel was such a great idea and took it for a test spin.

They got off at the next corner.

But Microsoft, being the brazen bunch on the block, pushed it down everyone's throat and said, use it because we don't have to support JAVA or JScript.

So, anyone using Windows had to use it.

{ came the law suits and Microsoft had to start learning how to play fair.

Still, a lot of people still use JScript even though JavaScript is still king of the hill. Mostly likely because it is JScript.

Well, that's the story on the street.

Fact is, Microsoft back in 1996 decided they needed two scripting languages: VBScript and JScript. One would be used for server-side scripting and the other on the client side.

While JScript can do both, it was given the green light to work with IIS, HTML and so forth.

Which left a bunch of confused Java programmers wondering why JScript? And that's the reason for the street story.

The truth is, both scripting languages can be used for all purposes.

What you are about to do is embark on a journey. While this may or may not land you a new job. It will certainly look good on your resume.

No one can force you to write code. The old saying of: "You can lead a horse to water, but you can't make it drink" is as true today as ever before.

So, my challenge is to make it interesting and fun as possible. If I succeed at that that I've succeeded at working with you to learn JScript.

Welcome to JScript

WHAT IS JSCRIPT?

Well, obviously, JScript is a Java based scripting language that was created by Microsoft back in 1996. The language is almost a carbon copy of JScript but because Microsoft didn't want to deal with Sun Microsystems and possible law suits Microsoft called it JScript.

Furthermore, JScripts shares the use of both CScript and WScript. Which means your scripts can run in both 32-bit mode and 64-bit mode and from inside a DOS Command Shell and from the desktop.

Right now, let's start with a humble beginning

We're not going to get very far without me talking about and providing you with the tools needed to learn this language, so...

Go to start, to run, type in Notepad and press enter. { type in your name, go to the menu on Notepad, click file, save and inside quotes, type Lesson1.js and save the file to your desktop. Should look like this.

Now double click on it and see what happens.

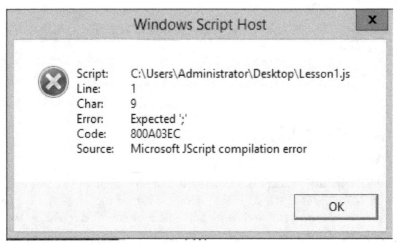

Notice the compiler is looking for ';'. Not what you expected if worked with the VBScript version.

Add a semi-colon to the end of your name and let's try again.

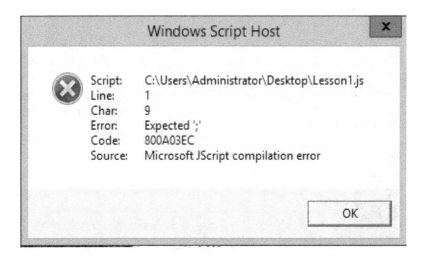

Same error. Did you spot why this happened again? There is a space between my First Name and my middle initial. So. let's put one there. And run it again.

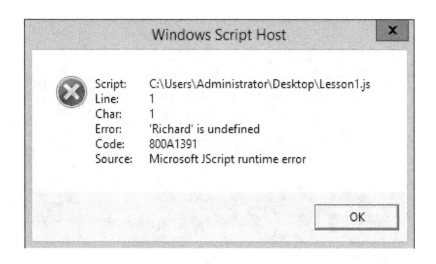

There are three reasons why you needed to do this.

First, your name was being parsed for key words and the scripting engine couldn't find your name in its list.

Second, it proves that you just can't write anything you please and expect the language to understand it.

Third, the error message was created using the WScript which means you aren't using a DOS Command window.

So, now, go to start, run, type in cmd and press enter. Once the DOS Command window is up and running, type in CScript and add a space right after the word. Drag and drop lesson1 into the DOS window and press enter.

See the difference here? CScript is used with DOS console type scripts while WScript is used when the program is being used in the windows environment. But I forced windows to use CScript. If I get rid of CScript, the same Windows Script Host message box about the error will show up with the same popup as previously shown.

For this reason, the CScript is your best choice when the script runs on someone else's machine and you've automated routines that aren't stopped by message boxes.

Key point to be made: CScript is used for console-based scripts while WScript is used for Windows.

Let's fix the lesson1 so it does more than cause errors. Open it up and type:
WScript.Echo(and your name in quotes)
And then save it and run it. When I do this with my name, this is what I get:

But is WScript. Echo the only way to let people know your program will talk back? Of course not. You can use:

```
var ws= new ActiveXObject('WScript.Shell');
ws.Popup(your name in quotes);
```

But I can assure you that some nut job is going to ask the following:

What are the three ways you can glean custom information from users and use it in your program.

And the answer should be:

Depends what is hosting JScript.

If it is HTML window.alert, window.confirm, window.prompt and WScript.Shell Popup.

If it is CScript or WScript, WScript.Echo or WScript.Shell Popup.

And you wouldn't be wrong.

If you are just running a 32-bit operating system, { this doesn't apply to you. But if your operating system is 64-bit, { you're going to need to know this. By default, you're running your scripts in 64-bit mode and since most of the programs you're planning on running use 32-bit, you're going to need to know how to run these in that mode.

So, by default, your 64-bit versions live in your Windows\System32 directory. That is where you will see CScript.exe and WScript.exe.

The 32-bit versions are in the Windows\SysWOW64 directory with exactly the same names: CScript.exe and WScript.exe.

So, how can you easily switch between them?

Follow the steps in the next chapter.

Getting Ready to Rumble

I HAVE SOME TASKS FOR YOU TO DO.

Task 1: Create a new folder for your JScript lessons on your desktop

Move you mouse over to an area on your desktop where there are no ICONS and use the right click button on your mouse to activate your desktop menu, slide your mouse pointer down to new and then slide it over to folder. Click on it and a new folder with the name New Folder will show up on your desktop.

Click on it and then use your right click muse button to activate the menu. Slide your mouse pointer down the list until you get to Rename. Click that and rename the folder to Simply JScript.

After you've done that, press enter.

Double click on the folder and it will open the blank folder up for you.

Task 2: Create two new folders inside your Simply JScript Folder

Open the new folder: Simply JScript. Right click inside the folder area and choose new and then folder. Name it 32-bit. Repeat the process and name the new folder 64-bit.

Task 3: Creating a Notepad shortcut

Again, Right click inside the folder area. Go down to where you see new. Once selected another menu will appear as it did when you created an new folder and just below it, you will see the word Shortcut.

A window will appear and ask you for the location and name of the file. Click browse. Go to your windows drive and click on Windows. Once you are in that directory, look for Notepad and click on it and then click okay. The window will return with the location of the file – which, you could have just copy and pasted this into the textbox:

C:\Windows\notepad.exe

Click next and then click Finish. You now have a shortcut that is easier to use then having to go to start, run and type in Notepad.

Task 4: Create a 64-bit DOS Command window

Open up the 64-bit folder and Repeat the same steps you did above to create the shortcut for Notepad, only this time, you're want to the below location:

C:\Windows\System32\cmd.exe

In fact, you can copy and paste the above into the textbox. Or just browse over to the windows folder { system 32 folder and then look for cmd.exe

Click next and then click Finish. You now have a shortcut for running the command console window.

Task 5: Create a 32-bit DOS Command window

Close the 64-bit folder and open the 32-bit folder. Repeat the process above but use the

C:\Windows\SysWOW64\cmd.exe for the path to the executable.

Click next. Name the file 32-bit cmd and click finish.

Task 6: Create a 32-bit Windows Script Host Helper Script.

Copy your notepad shortcut into both the 32-bit and 64-bit folders. { run the one in the 32 -bit folder and type the script in below:

```
var ws;
If WScript.Arguments.Length > 0
{
    ws = new ActiveXObject("WScript.Shell");
    ws.run("C:\\Windows\\sysWOW64\\WScript " + WScript.Arguments(0));
}
else
{
    WScript.Quit(-1);
```

}

Save this in the 32-bit folder and name it with quotes around it, "32bitWScriptRunner.js"

Close Notepad.

Congratulations! You have created folder and some shortcuts you can now call your JScript work space.

WScript.Arguments is a collection of Command line variables your script accepts. That doesn't mean you have to use it in your scripts, it simply means that you can create variables that need to be passed in and this is how they are dealt with on the command line.

Here's how it works.

```
if(WScript.Arguments.Length < 2)
{
    WScript.Echo("Please supply FirstName    MiddleInitial    LastName before clicking here");
    WScript.Quit(-1);
}
else
{
    WScript.Echo(WScript.Arguments(0) + " " + WScript.Arguments(1) + " " + WScript.Arguments(2))
}
```

Admittedly, there should be some error trapping to make sure the path and filename are correct. But it does get the job done.

And thinking about it, it does make sense to assure that the extension of the file is correct and the file exists.

So let's do that now.

```
var pos;
var ws;
var fso;
var tstr;

if WScript.Arguments.Length > 0 {
    fso = new ActiveXObject("Scripting.FileSystemObject");
    tstr = WScript.Arguments(0);
```

```
    tstr = trim(tstr);
     pos = instr(lCase(tstr), ".js");
    if pos == 0 {
       WScript.Quit(-1);
    }
    if fso.FileExists(tstr) == false {
      WScript.Quit(-1);
    }
    ws = new ActiveXObject("WScript.Shell");
    ws.run("C:\\Windows\\System32\\WScript " + WScript.Arguments(0));
}
```

Generally speaking, these arguments are made public and are based on the need of the script to perform the tasks contained within the script. Things like a computer name, what the script should be looking for, etc.

Aside from a configuration file, and interactive user prompts, this is the only direct way at the time the script is to run to pass in command line variables from outside the script as the script starts running. For certain, it is the only way a dynamically driven JScript can make Windows drag and drop functionality work. Isn't that exactly what you want to be able to do?

PROVING THE SWITCHING
WORKS

Go to your 32-bit directory and run your copy of Notepad from there. Type in the following:

```
var cn;
var dl;
cn = new ActiveXObject("ADODB.Connection");
dl = new ActiveXObject("DataLinks");
cn = dl.PromptNew();
```

Save it as Datalinks.js with quotes around it. Close Notepad. Now, double Click on the Datalinks.js and you should see:

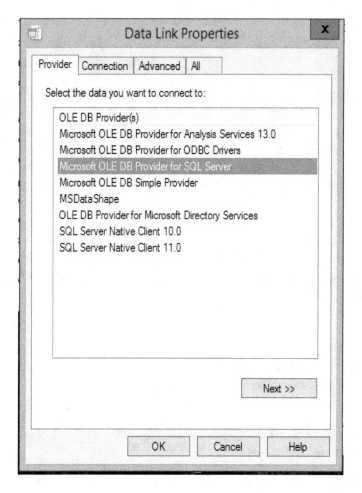

Now drag and drop the datalinks.js onto 32bitWScriptRunner.js and you should see this:

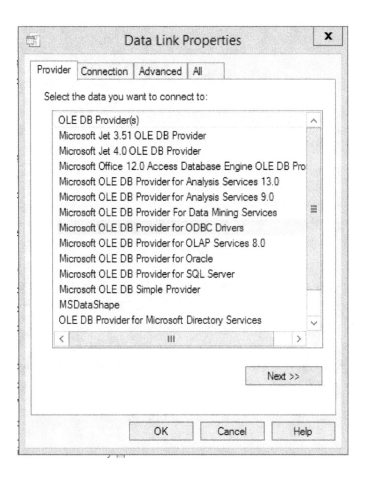

It is time to reflect on what I've done and why I've done it.

Okay, so far, I've established that there are two distinct of files on a 64-bit Operating System. The ones for 32-bit and the ones for 64-bit.

In order for us to work with both I made up folders and files to make working with these difference files much easier to do.

We also just saw the switching at work. It showed us proof there is a difference between the 32-bit version and the 64-bit version visually using the Datalinks.

Working with the Internet Explorer

W E – meaning you and me – are about to solve a problem. But first, the goal is to create a process that involves Internet explorer. There are a couple of ways you can run explorer from your desktop.

One, you can create a shortcut like the way you have been doing. But you still have to type in the web page once it is up.

Two, you can use WScript. Shell and use the run function:

```
var ws;

ws = new ActiveXObject("WScript.Shell");
ws.Run("HTTPS://www.Google.com") ;
```

Three, you can use InternetExplorer.Application class and create an instance of IE that way.

```
var ie;

ie = new ActiveXObject("InternetExplorer.Application");
ie.Visible = true;
ie.Navigate2("https://www.yahoo.com");
```

While these do work, to create an instance of IE, there are some issues with each that does make it hard for you to know when the object you created in code has ended.

Why would that even concern you, right?

It probably shouldn't. After all, the whole objective here is to start an instance if IE and tell it where you want to go.

But what if you needed to know exactly when the instance you created either stopped running or was shut down by the person using it?

As it turns out, JScript doesn't have a direct way to know when processes start and when they end. The script simply gets IE started and, well, is finished working after that point. It is known as the process going out of scope.

But what if you could? Below is one way of doing it.

```
var ie;
var ws;
var fso;

ie = new ActiveXObject("InternetExplorer.Application");
ie.Visible = true;
ie.Navigate2("https://www.yahoo.com");
WScript.Echo("Running.");

while(ie == "Internet Explorer")
{
   WScript.Sleep(250);
}
WScript.Echo("Explorer stopped running.");
```

Save this a Explorer.js. and then run it.

Did it work?

What you should see happen, is the ie code worked just fine. It isn't until you try being smart that loop that you get in trouble.

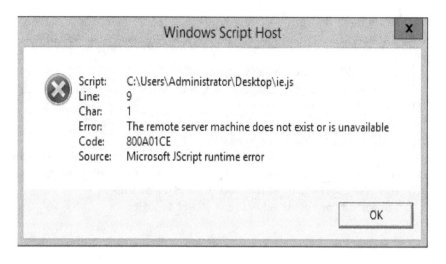

Why?

Simple, we're wanting to make sure that when ie is no longer around, you get notified. The problem is, the darn thing turns into a null!
So, you get an error.

Wow! Imagine my surprise!

There's two ways to resolve this error:

The first:

```
var ie;
var ws;
var fso;

ie = new ActiveXObject("InternetExplorer.Application");
ie.Visible = true;
ie.Navigate2("https://www.yahoo.com");
WScript.Echo("Running.");
try
{
   while(ie == "Internet Explorer")
   {
      WScript.Sleep(250);
```

```
    }
}
catch(err)
{

}
WScript.Echo("Explorer stopped running.");


Second:

var sink;
var ProcessID = 0;
var v
Sub sink_OnObjectReady(objWbemObject, objWbemAsyncContext)
{
  Switch(objWbemObject.Path_.Class)
  {
    case "__InstanceCreationEvent":
    {
        var obj = objWbemObject.Properties_.Item("TargetInstance").Value;
        if (obj.Properties_.Item("Name").Value == "iexplore.exe")
        {
          if (processID = 0)
          {
            ProcessID = obj.Properties_.Item("ProcessID").Value;
            WScript.Echo("Process has Started.");
          }
        }
        break;
    }
    case "__InstanceDeletionEvent":
    {
      var obj = objWbemObject.Properties_.Item("TargetInstance").Value;
      if (ProcessID == obj.Properties_.Item("ProcessID").Value)
      {
        WScript.Echo("Process has ended.");
        v=1;
      }
      break;
```

```
            }
        }
    }
    v=0
    svc = GetObject("Winmgmts:\\\.\\root\\cimv2");
    svc.Security_.AuthenticationLevel = 6;
    svc.Security_.ImpersonationLevel = 3;
    sink = WScript.CreateObject("WbemScripting.SWbemSink", "sink_");
    svc.ExecNotificationQueryAsync(sink, "SELECT * FROM
___InstanceOperationEvent WITHIN 1 WHERE TargetInstance ISA 'Win32_Process'
and TargetInstance.Name == 'iexplore.exe'");

    var ie = new ActiveXObject("InternetExplorer.Application");
    ie.Visible = true;
    ie.Navigate2("https://www.Google.com");
    while(v == 0)
    {
        WScript.Sleep(500);
    }
```

Never Believe everything at face value
Facts can be lies twisted into truths

B Below are a couple of them.

Well, that's what the purists say about everything until it really is broken out of the box.

Anyway. I would like you to create a blank JScript file for two reasons. One, because creating a script is just as easy as just saving a file and, two, you need to get used to putting quotes around

Open Notepad and save the file with Quotes around I as "Blank.js"

Once the file is created, you should see what looks like a light sea green icon on your desktop which appears to be a rolled up top and bottom making an S shape.

If you double click on it, nothing will happen. This is exactly where you want to start. With the notion that nothing is wrong with your code until you start writing it.

Did that make you smile? I hope so. Code isn't broken when there is no code written with faulty logic or assumptions that are not true.

Never cut and paste code from here

If you don't believe me, just try this:

Open Notepad, copy the following: ms = new ActiveXObject("MSXM2.DomDocuement") and paste it into Notepad and save the file with Quotes around I as "WhyItWillNotWork.js". Now, run it.

Windows Script Host

C:\Users\Administrator\Desktop\Newfolder\WhyIrWillNotWork.js

Line: 1

Char: 23

Error: Invalid character

Code: 800A0408

Source: Microsoft JScript compilation error

Honestly, you can't even cut and paste the name from here either. You need to type it in by hand and add the quotes. But don't worry, I have a couple of surprises for you, soon and I think these are going to really make your day.

Code you can have fun tinkering with
I never said you can't have fun with code

B ELOW, ARE SOME THINGS YOU CAN DO

DOING SOME HARD TIME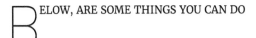

Open Notepad.
Type this in: WScript.Echo(Time)
Save the file with Quotes around I as "Time.js"
Once the file is created, double click on it. A window will popup telling you the current time.

WHAT DAY IS IT?

Open Notepad.
Type this in: WScript.Echo(Day)
Save the file with Quotes around I as "Day.js"
Once the file is created, double click on it. A window will popup telling you the current day.

12 Keys To The Kingdom

Every Language that supports COM enables you

to do these

There are 12 lines of code types used today in every language that supports COM based programming. These are:

1. The creation of an object
2. The use of a property to get\set a value
3. The use of a function that does or does not accept parameters and may or may not return a value. Functions are also called methods.
4. The use of an event that occurs and you write code to respond to it.
5. The use of enumerators
6. The use of conditional Loops
7. The use of conditional branches
8. The use of error trapping
9. Data Conversions
10. Constants
11. Declarations
12. Reg Expressions

Let's take a look at each.

Every language that works with Windows and Office products has a way to communicate with them. In JScript, this is done two ways.

The words here that are used are new ActiveXObject and GetObject.

new ACTIVEXOBJECT

So, what is new ActiveXObject? The sugar-coated answer is that it creates something that can be used to perform a task. In-other-words, if Office is installed, and you typed:

var oWord = new ActiveXObject("Word.Application");

Once, you've created the object, you have a way to communicate with it.

oWord.Visible = true;

new ActiveXObject was modified back around 2000 to include the ability to connect to a remote machine. With all the security and firewalls in place, it is doubtful that would be worth trying today.

GetObject

GetObject is old school. Used to be a time when you could use it for a lot of different things. It works like CreateObject in that you can create an object but is primarily used today with Winmgmts and WinNT.

var svc = GetObject("winmgmts:\\\\.\\root\\cimv2");

Again, once you've created the object, you can use the object reference.

svc.Security_.AuthenticationLevel =6;

Please don't try these. They are examples that do work. You'll be able to see them in action much later. There is a lot more to in order to make the above code segments worth your while using.

Besides, creating objects is the fun and easy part of this truly fascinating journey. And like any puzzle, every part that will be covered here is one step closer to completing it.

The use of a property to get\set a value

Properties can be something that you create or something that has already been created for you.

If for example, you decided that a property needed to be   like shown in the above example to 6:

svc.Security_.AuthenticationLevel =6;

Okay, so how do you find out what the property was before I changed it?

var old;

old = svc.Security_.AuthenticationLevel;

Yes, it is just that simple.

What if you wanted to create your own property?

Set it:

var myproperty = 25;

Get it:

var old = myproperty;

Okay, so why would you want to a property to 25 knowing getting the property would return 25? Well, there are situations where a return value would tell you whether or not something returned with a return value that was greater than zero and if checked, whether or not the call worked

var iret = ws.Run("Notepad.exe");

What is a method?

A method is a sub or function that can be created by the program to perform a task or called by your program to perform a task that the calling program knows is available and knows how to use it.

Technically, the creation of an object falls under the category of a method as it is a function that returns a value. It is only highlighted a key to the kingdom because of its importance to writing a program.

It is also a way in which zero or more properties can be passed in. These can be for private or public and they can be a function or a sub.

Function example:

```
function GetValue(Name,  obj)
{
    Return;
}
```

Sub example:

```
sub Value( name, obj)
```

```
{

}
```

When calling a sub or function, unless it is specified as being an optional value, all properties must be satisfied otherwise, the function or sub will either not work or raise an error.

For example, when the below code is called in this manner, it still works:

```
var l = new ActiveXObject("WbemScripting.SWbemLocator");
var svc = l.ConnectServer();
```

Despite the fact that there are 8 variables that can be passed in:

```
var svc = locator.ConnectServer(".",   "root\\cimV2", Username, Password,
Locale, Authority, Security Flags, SWbemNamedValue)
```

The reason for these properties being up this way was simple, unless you are trying to connect to a remote machine, UserName and Password would cause an error. Unless you are going to the default namespace: root\cimV2; and planning on using one of the classes: Win32_LogicalDisk, for example, if the class you are wanting to use is located elsewhere other than the default, you have to specify it before you attempt to use that class.

Events YOU CAN respond to it

Windows in an event driven environment and as such, your JScript program can create event routines which tell you something has happened and you can respond to it. Here's an example of an event you can create in code that was created in JScript that works:

```
var v = 0;
Sub sink_OnObjectReady(ByVal objWbemObject, ByVal objWbemAsyncContext)
{
    var propEnum = new Enumerator(objWbemObject.Properties_);
    for (;!propEnum.atEnd(); propEnum.moveNext())
    {
        v = v + prop.Name+ " " + GetValue(prop.Name, objWbemObject)+ vbCrLf
    }
    WScript.Echo(v);
}
```

This is called an Async Event call because the program can perform other tasks while waiting for this event to fire off asynchronously.

The problem is, scripts don't just sit around waiting for events to happen isn't what the script likes to do. It likes to do what it needs to perform the task at hand and exit. And that's where I use a bit of WScript magic.

```
while(w == 0)
{
  WScript.Sleep(500)
}
```

When the Async call, in this case, is completed, the controller of the event raises an event called OnCompleted:

```
Sub            sink_OnCompleted(iHResult,           objWbemErrorObject,
objWbemAsyncContext)
{
  w = 1;
}
```

And when this happens the loop that keeps the script running, reads the change in w and knows a w=1 means it is done and the code moves on to do whatever else is left to do.

Also, in some cases Async calls don't need an event function to happen.

Here's another example:

```
var es = Svc.ExecNotificationQuery("Select * From ___InstanceCreationEvent
WITHIN 1 where TargetInstance ISA 'Win32_Process'")
while(w < 5)
{
    var ti = es.NextEvent(-1);
    var obj = ti.Properties_.Item("TargetInstance").Value;
    var propset = obj.Properties_;
    var propEnum = new Enumerator(propset);
    for (; !propEnum.atEnd(); propEnum.moveNext())
    {
        v = v + prop.Name + " " + GetValue(prop.Name, obj) + '\n';
    }
    WScript.Echo(v);
      w=w+1;
}
```

This may appear as though it is not asynchronous, but if you consider the pattern, you can see that the notification isn't just doing it once, it is doing it 4 times and is responding to the event as it happens. And not because you want it to happen 4 times.

The use of enumerators

Technically speaking there are two of these that JScript uses. For Each and For
For(var x=0; x < rs.Fields.Count; x++)
{

}
var propEnum = new Enumerator(propset);
for (; !propEnum.atEnd(); propEnum.moveNext())
{
    v = v + prop.Name + " " + GetValue(prop.Name, obj) + '\n';
}
These are technically non-conditional enumerators because they are not based
on a conditional which must be proven to be true of false.

For Each is based on a enumerating through as collection of objects. You will
be seeing a lot of this kind of enumerator when I work with WBemScripting because
the objects collection and the properties collection are a natural fit for this kind of
information processing.

The For is also ideal for use with a Fields Count and RecordCount because there
is an indexer involved and that allows for easy processing of the information. Unlike
For Each, where the collection simply needs to be enumerated through, this also
allows us to go to each column and row as a specifically, chosen position rather than
blindly look for something in a collection.

For also works with other forms of collected data when working with XML and
enumerating through a nodelist, Child Nodes, and Attribute Nodes. Since these too
are also index driven.

The use of conditional Loops

There are six conditional loops
while(Some condition)
{

}

do
{

}
while(Some condition)

These two loops are basically contradictory of each other. The first checks the condition before and while the loop is being used. The second doesn't until after the loop is used and continues doing so until the condition is met.

The use of conditional branches

Below are conditional branches. Generally speaking these can be stand alone or placed inside a loop.

```
if
{
}

if
{
}
else
{
}

if
{
}
else if
{
}
else
{
}
```

As an example, below is one of our favorites (in the VB languages):

```
var tstr = Object.Path_.Classname;
var pos = tstr.indexOf ( "_");
```

What this does is tell me where the _ is located in a Classname. There are three possible scenarios:

1. There are no _.
2. There is one at the very beginning.
3. There is one in the middle.

```
if (pos == -1)
```

```
{
}
else if (pos == 0)
{
}
else
{
}
```

This is exactly the logic I needed to parse the three possible incomes from what I knew was going to happen when looking for three specific possibilities. But this only works when the last else is basically a catch all.

Best in the world is try catch finally. I'm just happy with try and catch.
Looks like this:

```
try
{

}
catch (err)
{

}
```

Here's an interesting one according to the documentation, using Boolean with a value is supposed to return a 0 for false and a -1 for true. So if v = 0, it returns a 0 because the value is 0 and is supposed to return false. False as in 0 not an actual false.

So, I ran this:

```
var v=0;
var iret = Boolean(v);
WScript.Echo(iret);
```

And it returned:

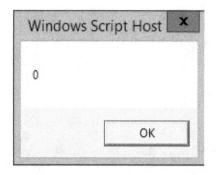

Then I ran this:

```
var v=1;
var iret = Boolean(v);
WScript.Echo(iret);
```

And it returned this:

So, logically, I tried this next:

```
var v=0;
var iret = Boolean(v);

switch(iret)
{
  case 0:
  {
    WScript.Echo("false");
    break;
  }
}
```

```
  case -1:
  {
    WScript.Echo("true");
    break;
  }
}
```

Well, that didn't work. Which perplexed me since I did see the numbers as I should you on the popups I captured. After all, the return values do look like integers and the switch statement should have seen them as integers. So, I said, throw everything away to chance and try false and true and see what happens.

As it turned out, that worked. But I'm still not sure why what I was seeing physically was being converted under the hood to something other than a 0 and a -1.

```
var v=1;
var iret = Boolean(v);
switch(iret)
{
  case false:
  {
    WScript.Echo("false");
    break;
  }
  case true:
  {
    WScript.Echo("true");
    break;
  }
}
```

This still leaves me scratching my head because, this wasn't documented and the documentation that was available implied that the return value was 0 or -1 and that needed to be interrupted as being true or false.

Constants

Constants are static values and can be in various formats including Hex and Long.

```
var wbemFlagReturnImmediately = 0x10;
```

```
var wbemFlagForwardOnly = 0x20;
```

These two could just as easily be written like this:

```
var wbemFlagReturnImmediately = 16;
var wbemFlagForwardOnly = 32;
```

Declarations

I've pretty well covered this. When you var – short for Gremlins – a variable, by default it is a variant and I've already shown you how.

```
var strQuery;
strQuery = "Select * from Products";
```

or:

```
var strQuery = "Select * from Products";
```

Reg Expressions

Regular expressions - Reg Expressions – are ways in which you can replace string values and validate strings.

Regular Expressions

When you combine all the previously mentioned "keys to the kingdom", you pretty much have all the pieces needed to create almost any program

CHAPTER TITLE

Chapter Subtitle

Chapter Epigraph uses a quote or verse to
introduce the chapter and set the stage.
—Attribute the quote

Take a look at my parsing routine:

```
function GetValue(Name, obj)
{
    var tempstr = new String();
    var tempstr1 = new String();
    var tName = new String();
    tempstr1 = obj.GetObjectText_();
    var re = /"/g;
    tempstr1 = tempstr1.replace(re , "");
    var pos;
    tName = Name + " = ";
    pos = tempstr1.indexOf(tName);
    if (pos > -1)
    {
        pos = pos + tName.length;
        tempstr = tempstr1.substring(pos, tempstr1.length);
```

```
pos = tempstr.indexOf(";");
tempstr = tempstr.substring(0, pos);
tempstr = tempstr.replace("{", "");
tempstr = tempstr.replace("}", "");
if (tempstr.length > 13)
{
    if (obj.Properties_(Name).CIMType == 101)
    {
        tempstr = tempstr.substr(4, 2) + "/"  + tempstr.substr(6, 2) + "/" +
tempstr.substr(0, 3) + " " + tempstr.substr(8, 2) + ":" + tempstr.substr(10, 2) + ":" +
tempstr.substr(12, 2);
    }
}
return tempstr;
}
else
{
    return "";
}
}
```

While there are a few I don't use in this parsing routine, these are the ones I need to make my routine work correctly. With the point being, find the rest on the internet and learn what each one does. These are, after, all your tools that enable you to accomplish tasks.

Creating Arrays

Okay, so here's the idea. Arrays are places where you can store information.

```
var x;
var y;
var Names();
var Values(,);

Names(rs.Fields.count);
Values(rs.RecordCount, rs.Fields.count);
```

This is the way I can create two arrays to hold the names of my fields and the values of my fields when I'm wanting to enumerate through a record.

The routine would look like this:

```
y=0
While(rs.EOF == false)
{
    for (x=0; x < rs.Fields.count; x++)
    {
      if y== 0
      {
         Names(x) = rs.Fields(x).Names;
         Values(y, x) = rs.Fields(x).Value;
      }
      else
```

```
    {
        Values(y, x) == rs.Fields(x).Value;
    }
    rs.MoveNext();
    y=y+1;
}
```

Some tantalizing Tidbits

BELOW, ARE SOME GOOD TO KNOW FACTS ABOUT JSCRIPT

There are ways in which you can compare things. These, in VB are the following:

== equals

< less than

> greater than

!= not equal to

<= equal to and less than

=> equal to and greater than

Open Notepad and type this:

'Just another way to let your users know something has happened.

```
var ws = new ActiveXObject("WScript.Shell");
ws.Run("Https://www.Bing.com");
ws.Run("Https://www.Facebook.com");
ws.Run("Https://www.Google.com");
ws.Run("Https://www.Yahoo.com");
```

Save the file as "FavoriteSites.js". Once the file is created, double click on it. Whatever your default browser is, it should come up and display all the sites each in a separate tab.

WScript.Shell Explained

This particular object is probably one of the most powerful one. Especially for us. For a wide variety of reasons.

1. The ws.CurrentDirectory is used in almost all of the examples.
2. Getting a list of Special Folders will help us later on
3. SendKeys can automate workflows
4. Run will be used to start Access and Excel and pull in a CSV text file
5. Popup will also be used later
6. CreateShortCut is a great way to place files on a user's desktop

That is 6 of 14 we're going to be using in this book.

With that said, let's dive into the deep end.

AppActivate

Best way to describe this one is it is a cool kind of weird.

Okay, so what's happening here? Well, first off, AppActivate assumes that everything it should find is based on the parent: JScript's console window existence. So, if you already have an Access Application up before doing this, they don't exist.

So, even if you have MSAccess running, it won't see it. It will return false no matter what.

Now, I create an instance of Access by running the ws.RunCommand: ws.Run("MSAccess")

And that brings up a new instance of Access.

Open Notepad.

Type this in:

```
var ws = new ActiveXObject("WScript.Shell");
ws.appActivate("Microsoft Access");
```

Save the file as AppactivateAccess.js and then run it. Access is again, the window commanding our attention. In-other-words, the method works to bring the window to the forefront.

CreateShortCut

Open Notepad and type this in:

```
var ws = new ActiveXObject("WScript.Shell");
var nl = ws.CreateShortcut("C:\\users\\Administrator\\Desktop\\ie.lnk");
nl.TargetPath = "C:\\Program Files (x86)\\Internet Explorer\\iexplore.exe";
nl.Arguments = "";
nl.Description = "32-bit Internet Explorer";
nl.WindowStyle = "1";
nl.WorkingDirectory = "C:\\Program Files (x86)\\Internet Explorer";
nl.Save();
nl = null;
```

Save the file as 32bitIEShortcut.js and then run it.
A link for 32-bit IE is on your desktop.

EXEC

Works almost exactly like the Run version.

Open Notepad and type this in:

```
ws = new ActiveXObject("WScript.Shell")
ws.exec("Calc")
```

Save the file as calc.js and then run it. A Calculator will appear on the desktop.

ExpandEdenvironmentsettings

Ever wanted to know what is ExpandedEnvironmentSettings?

Open Notepad and type this in:

```
var ws = new ActiveXObject(" WScript.Shell");
var fullpath = ws.ExpandEnvironmentStrings("%windir%, 0"):
ws.Popup (fullpath):
```

Save the file as windowsPath.js and then run it. A popup will tell you the windows directory.

I suppose your biggest question is, why would I want to log an event? The fact is, logging an event is a great way to let others know that you were on a machine and your program launched on a certain day in time.

But there's more to it { that. This also a way you can tell technical support about an error you've encountered trying to run your script.

Eventlog severity levels are the following:

```
 0  SUCCESS
 1  ERROR
 2  WARNING
 4  INFORMATION
 8  AUDIT_SUCCESS
16  AUDIT_FAILURE
```

Open Notepad and type this in:

```
var ws = new ActiveXObject("WScript.Shell");
ws.LogEvent(4, "You started reading this book!");
Save the file as AddEvent.js and then run it.
```

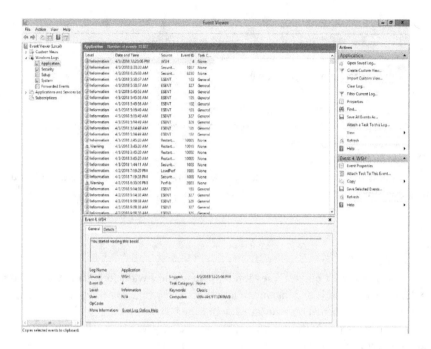

Believe me when I tell you this, you'll be back!

Popup

Just another way to let your users know something has happened.

Open Notepad and type in:

```
var ws = new ActiveXObject("WScript.Shell");
ws.Popup( "You struck gold");
```
Save the file as Youstruckgold.js and then run it. A message will pop up on the screen.

RegDelete, RegRead, RegWrite

I am not going to show you RegDelete or RegWrite. If you want to learn how to use those two, please feel free to do it on your own.

As for RegRead:

Open Notepad and type in:

```
var key = "HKEY_CLASSES_ROOT\MDACVer.Version\CurVer\"
var ws = new ActiveXObject("WScript.Shell")
var retstr = ws.RegRead(key)
ws.Popup(retstr);
```

Save the file as MDACCurrentVersion.js and then run it. A message will pop up on the screen telling you what version of MDAC you're running on your computer.

Run

Open Notepad and type in:

```
Works almost exactly like the exec  version.
var ws = new ActiveXObject("WScript.Shell");
ws.Run("MSPaint");
```

Save the file as Open Paint.js and then run it. Paint should start running.

Sendkeys

Sendkeys is about the most cantankerous method that you will want to use. First, the program where you want to send the keys to has to be running and the active window. If you decide to use hot keys, the other program needs to be able to use them.

Open Notepad and type in:

```
var ws = new ActiveXObject("WScript.Shell");
ws.Run("Excel");
ws.Sleep(500);
ws.SendKeys("Why did you wait this long to send me?");

ws.Run("Notepad");
ws.Sleep(500);
ws.SendKeys("Wait, you forgot me!");
```

Save the file as Open sendkeys.js and then run it. The two different programs should start running and the messages get type into the programs.

CurrentDirectory

You would be surprised to know just how many people don't know the Current Directory works both ways. You can get and set it as shown below:

```
ws = new ActiveXObject("WScript.Shell")
WScript.Echo(ws.CurrentDirectory)

ws.CurrentDirectory = "C:\"
WScript.Echo(ws.CurrentDirectory)
```

Special Folders

Ever wonder what are special folders and how do you get to them?
No?
Neither did I.

But the the code below will reveal them to you.
```
var v
var ws = new ActiveXObject("WScript.Shell")
var sf = ws.SpecialFolders

  v= v + s+ "\n";
}
WScript.Echo(v)
```

Below, is what JScript returns:

C:\Users\Public\Desktop
C:\ProgramData\Microsoft\Windows\Start Menu
C:\ProgramData\Microsoft\Windows\Start Menu\Programs
C:\ProgramData\Microsoft\Windows\Start Menu\Programs\StartUp
C:\Users\Administrator\Desktop
C:\Users\Administrator\AppData\Roaming
C:\Users\Administrator\AppData\Roaming\Microsoft\Windows\Printer Shortcuts
C:\Users\Administrator\AppData\Roaming\Microsoft\Windows\Templates

C:\Windows\Fonts

C:\Users\Administrator\AppData\Roaming\Microsoft\Windows\Network Shortcuts

C:\Users\Administrator\Desktop

C:\Users\Administrator\AppData\Roaming\Microsoft\Windows\Start Menu

C:\Users\Administrator\AppData\Roaming\Microsoft\Windows\SendTo

C:\Users\Administrator\AppData\Roaming\Microsoft\Windows\Recent

C:\Users\Administrator\AppData\Roaming\Microsoft\Windows\Start Menu\Programs\Startup

C:\Users\Administrator\Favorites

C:\Users\Administrator\Documents

C:\Users\Administrator\AppData\Roaming\Microsoft\Windows\Start Menu\Programs

Now that I've gone through all of what WScript.Shell object model has to offer, it is time to take your job expertise to the next level.

Since the coding for various Objects is defined and dictated by the object itself, there's little room for creativity and flexibility.

WS.Network Explained

When you don't know what an object is capable of, how can you fully uses all of the resources JScript is capable of doing? Obviously, you can't. So, when I find something I think you're going to want to use, I'm going to show you things like the below table and then, I'm going to show you how to use them.

What's my computer Name

Open Notepad and type this in:

```
var wn = new ActiveXObject("WScript.Network");
WScript.Echo(wn.ComputerName);
```

Save the file with Quotes around I as "ComputerName.js" And Double Click on it.

A window will popup telling you the Computer Name.

What's My Organization

Open Notepad and type this in:

```
var wn = new ActiveXObject("WScript.Network");
WScript.Echo(wn.Organization);
```

Save the file with Quotes around I as "Organization.js"

Once the file is created, double click on it. A window will popup telling you the organization your computer belongs to.

WHAT'S THE NAME OF MY SITE

Open Notepad and type this in:

```
wn = new ActiveXObject("WScript.Network");
WScript.Echo(wn.Site);
```

Save the file with Quotes around I as "Site.js"

Once the file is created, double click on it. A window will popup telling you the name of your site.

WHAT'S MY USERDOMAIN

Open Notepad and type this in:

```
var wn = new ActiveXObject("WScript.Network");
WScript.Echo(wn.UserDomain);
```

Save the file with Quotes around I as "Domain.js"
Once the file is created, double click on it. A window will popup telling you the Domain.

WHAT's MY USERNAME

Open Notepad type this in:

```
var wn = new ActiveXObject("WScript.Network");
WScript.Echo(wn.UserName);
```

Save the file with Quotes around I as "UserName.js"

Once the file is created, double click on it. A window will popup displaying your name.

WHAT's MY USERPROFILE

Open Notepad and type this in:

```
var wn = new ActiveXObject("WScript.Network");
WScript.Echo(wn.UserProfile);
```

Save the file with Quotes around I as "UserProfile.js"

Once the file is created, double click on it. A window will popup displaying your name.

THE VARIOUS WAYS TO DISPLAY INFORMATION

Open Notepad and type this:

```
var ws = new ActiveXObject("WScript.Shell");
WScript.Echo("Hello World");
ws.Popup("Hello World!");
```

Save the file as "HelloWorld.js".

Once the file is created, double click on it. A window will popup telling you Hello World.

The Scripting Object

I t isn't built directly into JScript, but it is something you'll be using quite often.

The Scripting Object is a suite of tools which helps you to perform tasks that involve Drives, Folders, Files and creating and writing information out to files.

BuildPath

The Build Path Function Returns a path and name combination. Below is an example of how it is used:

```
var fso;
var bp;
var Name;

Name = "Microsoft";
fso = new ActiveXObject("Scripting.FileSystemObject");
bp = fso.BuildPath("D:\", Name);
WScript.Echo (bp)
```

Note: This doesn't create the actual folder, it simply shows you how the path should look.

CopyFile

The CopyFile Function Copies a File from one location to another. Below is an example of how it is used:

```
var fso;
var Source;
var Destination;

Source = "C:\\Users\\Administrator\\Destkop\\bMatch.js";
Destination = "D:\Homeland\";

fso = new ActiveXObject("Scripting.FileSystemObject");
try
{
   bp = fso.CopyFile(Source, Destination, true);
   WScript.Echo("Copy file succeeded.");
}
catch(err)
{
    WScript.Echo("Copy file failed.");
}
```

CopyFolder

The CopyFolder Function Copies a Folder from one location to another. Below is an example of how it is used:

```
var bp;
var fso;
var Source;
var Destination;

Source = "C:\\Homeland";
Destination = "D:\\Users\\Administrator\\Desktop";
 fso = new ActiveXObject("Scripting.FileSystemObject");
bp = fso.CopyFolder(Source, Destination, 1);

try
{
   bp = fso.CopyFolder(Source, Destination, 1);
   WScript.Echo("Copy Folder succeeded.");
}
catch(err)
```

```
{
    WScript.Echo("Copy Folder failed.");
}
```

CreateFolder

The CreateFolder Function creates a Folder from a known path. Below is an example of how it is used:

```
var fso;
var bp;

fso = new ActiveXObject("Scripting.FileSystemObject");
try
{
    bp = fso.CreateFolder("C:\\Users\\Administrator\\Desktop\\HopeChest");
    WScript.Echo("Create Folder succeeded.");
}
catch(err)
{
    WScript.Echo("Create Folder failed.");
}
```

CreateTextFile

The CreateTextFile function creates a text file in a known folder. Below is how it works:
```
var fso;
var bp;

fso = new ActiveXObject("Scripting.FileSystemObject")

try
{
    bp = fso.CreateTextFile("C:\\Warren.txt", 1);
    WScript.Echo("CreateTextFile  succeeded.");
}
catch(err)
{
```

```
        WScript.Echo("CreateTextFile failed.");
}
```

DeleteFile

The CreateTextFile function creates a text file in a known folder. Below is how it works:

```
var fso;
var bp;

fso = new ActiveXObject("Scripting.FileSystemObject")
try
{
    bp = fso.DeleteFile("C:\\Warren.txt", 1);
    WScript.Echo("DeleteFile  succeeded.");
}
catch(err)
{
    WScript.Echo("DeleteFile failed.");
}
```

DeleteFolder

The DeleteFolder Function deletes a folder and contents from a known path. Below is an example of how it is used:

```
var fso;

fso = new ActiveXObject("Scripting.FileSystemObject");
try
{
    fso.DeleteFolder("C:\\Users\\Administrator\\Desktop\\Homeland");
    WScript.Echo("Delete Folder  succeeded.");
}
catch(err)
{
    WScript.Echo("Delete Folder failed.");
}
```

DriveExists

Used to determine if a drive exists. Below is an example of it in use:

```
var fso;

fso = new ActiveXObject("Scripting.FileSystemObject")
if(fso.DriveExists("z"))
{
   WScript.Echo ("This drive exists");
}
else
{
   WScript.Echo ("This drive does not exist");
}
```

FileExists

Used to determine if a file exists. Below is an example of it in use:

```
var fso;

fso = new ActiveXObject("Scripting.FileSystemObject");
If fso.FileExists("C:\\Users\\Administrator\\Desktop\\bMatch.js")
{
    WScript.Echo ("This file exists");
}
else
{
   WScript.Echo("This file does not exist");
}
```

FolderExists

Used to determine if a folder exists. Below is an example of it in use:

```
var fso;
```

```
fso = new ActiveXObject("Scripting.FileSystemObject")
if(fso.FolderExists("C:\\Users\\Administrator\\Desktop")
{
    WScript.Echo("This folder exists");
else
{
    WScript.Echo("This folder does not exist");
}
```

GetAbsolutePathName

GetAbsolutePathName is used to find out where the script is running. Below is an example of it in use:

```
var fso;
var bp;

fso = new ActiveXObject("Scripting.FileSystemObject")
bp = fso.GetAbsolutePathName("c:")

WScript.Echo(bp);
```

GetBaseName

GetBaseName is used to return just the name of the file. Below is an example of it in use:

```
var fso;
var bp;

fso = new ActiveXObject("Scripting.FileSystemObject");
bp = fso.GetBaseName("c:\\Users\\Administrator\\Desktop\\bMatch.js");

WScript.Echo(bp);
```

GetDrive

GetDrive is used to reference a Drive and use that to enumerate folders and files on that drive. Below is an example of it in use:

```
var fso;
var bp;

 fso = new ActiveXObject("Scripting.FileSystemObject")
 bp = fso.GetDrive("c:\")

WScript.Echo(bp);
```

GetDriveName

GetDriveName is used to get the name from a specified file path. Below is an example of it in use:

```
var fso;
var bp;

fso = new ActiveXObject("Scripting.FileSystemObject");
bp = fso.GetDriveName("c:\users\Administrator\Desktop\bMatch.js");

WScript.Echo(bp);
```

GetExtensionName

GetExtensionName is used to get the name of the extension from a specified file path. Below is an example of it in use:

```
var fso;
var bp;

fso = new ActiveXObject("Scripting.FileSystemObject");
bp = fso.GetExtensionName("c:\users\Administrator\Desktop\bMatch.js");

WScript.Echo(bp);
```

GetFile

GetFile is used to get a reference a file that exists and display its properties. Below is an example of it in use:

```
var fso;
var bp;

fso = new ActiveXObject("Scripting.FileSystemObject");
```

You need to specify the file, the one I used here doesn't exist on your machine.

```
bp = fso.GetFile("c:\myfile.txt");
```

```
WScript.Echo(bp);
```

GetFileName

GetFileName function returns the name of a specified file. Below, is an example of it in use:

```
var fso;
var bp;

fso = new ActiveXObject("Scripting.FileSystemObject")
```

You need to specify the file, the one I used here doesn't exist on your machine.

```
bp = fso.GetFileName("c:\\users\\Administrator\\Desktop\\bMatch.js");
WScript.Echo(bp);
```

GetFileVersion

The GetFileVersion returns the version of a specified file. Below, is an example of it in use:

```
var fso;
var bp;

fso = new ActiveXObject("Scripting.FileSystemObject");
bp = fso.GetFileVersion("c:\users\Administrator\Desktop\bMatch.js");
```

```
WScript.Echo(bp);
```

GetFolder

GetFolder is used to reference a folder and can be used to enumerate sub-folders and files in that folder. Below is an example of it in use:

```
var fso;
var bp;
var fldr;

fso = new ActiveXObject("Scripting.FileSystemObject");
bp = fso.GetFolder("c:\");

WScript.Echo(bp);
```

GetParentFolderName

The GetParentFolderName function returns the parent folder. Below is an example of is use:

```
var fso;
var bp;
var fldr;

fso = new ActiveXObject("Scripting.FileSystemObject");
bp = fso.GetParentFolderNamer("c:\\Program Files");

WScript.Echo(bp);
```

GetSpecialFolder

This function can tell you what the Windows, System or temporary folder name is. Below is an example of its use:

```
var fso;
var bp;

fso = new ActiveXObject("Scripting.FileSystemObject");
```

Windows:

```
bp = fso.GetSpecialFolder(0);
```

System:

```
bp = fso.GetSpecialFolder(1)
```

Temp:

```
bp = fso.GetSpecialFolder(2);

WScript.Echo(bp);
```

GetTempName

GetTempName is a function that returns a temporary name that can { be used as a way to create a file. Below is an example of it being used:

```
var fso;
var bp;

fso = new ActiveXObject("Scripting.FileSystemObject");
bp = fso.GetTempName();

WScript.Echo(bp);
```

MoveFile

The MoveFile Function moves a file from a known path to another known path. Below is an example of how it is used:

```
var fso;
var bp;
var source;
var destination;
```

```
fso = new ActiveXObject("Scripting.FileSystemObject");

try
{
   bp = fso.MoveFile(Source, Destination, true);
   WScript.Echo("Move file succeeded.");
}
catch(err)
{
    WScript.Echo("Move file failed.");
}
```

MoveFolder

The MoveFolder Function moves a Folder from a known path to another known path. Below is an example of how it is used:

```
var fso;
var bp;
var source;
var destination;

fso = new ActiveXObject("Scripting.FileSystemObject");
try
{
   bp = fso.MoveFolder(Source, Destination);
   WScript.Echo("Move folder succeeded.");
}
Catch(err)
{
    WScript.Echo("Move folder failed.");
}
```

OpenTextFile

OpenTextFile is used to read, write and append a text file. Below is an example of it in use:

```
var fso;
```

var txtstream;

For reading:

```
fso = new ActiveXObject("Scripting.FileSystemObject");
txtstream   = fso.OpenTextFile("c:\Uses\Administrator\Desktop\myfile.txt", 1,
false, -2);
```

For writing:

```
fso = new ActiveXObject("Scripting.FileSystemObject");
txtstream   = fso.OpenTextFile("c:\Uses\Administrator\Desktop\myfile.txt", 2,
true, -2);
```

For appending:

```
fso = new ActiveXObject("Scripting.FileSystemObject");
txtstream   = fso.OpenTextFile("c:\Uses\Administrator\Desktop\myfile.txt", 8,
true, -2);
```

And there you have it. A rather long but important group of functions you can use in your JScript Programs.

Stylesheets
Do you proud every time

Stylesheets aren't just to make a page look
remarkable, they also make you look remarkable,
too.
— R. T. Edwards

What is the first thing you see when you go to a website and look at the home page for the first time? It is the level of professionalism – that keen insight to attention to details – that draws you in. Speaks to you. Tells you that the site wants you to stay a while and shares with you a common ground.

The unseen hero – css. I've created some stylesheets—listed below—so you can try and use with the various web related programs.

NONE

```
txtstream.WriteLine("<style type='text/css'>")
txtstream.WriteLine("th")
txtstream.WriteLine("")
txtstream.WriteLine("    COLOR: white;")
txtstream.WriteLine(" Next")
txtstream.WriteLine("td")
txtstream.WriteLine("")
txtstream.WriteLine("    COLOR: white;")
txtstream.WriteLine(" Next")
txtstream.WriteLine("</style>")
```

BLACK AND WHITE TEXT

```
txtstream.WriteLine("<style type='text/css'>")
txtstream.WriteLine("th")
txtstream.WriteLine("")
txtstream.WriteLine("    COLOR: white;")
txtstream.WriteLine("    BACKGROUND-COLOR: black;")
txtstream.WriteLine("    FONT-FAMILY: Cambria, serif;")
txtstream.WriteLine("    FONT-SIZE: 12px;")
txtstream.WriteLine("    text-align: left;")
txtstream.WriteLine("    white-Space: nowrap;")
txtstream.WriteLine(" Next")
txtstream.WriteLine("td")
txtstream.WriteLine("")
```

```
txtstream.WriteLine("    COLOR: white;")
txtstream.WriteLine("    BACKGROUND-COLOR: black;")
txtstream.WriteLine("    FONT-FAMILY: Cambria, serif;")
txtstream.WriteLine("    FONT-SIZE: 12px;")
txtstream.WriteLine("    text-align: left;")
txtstream.WriteLine("    white-Space: nowrap;")
txtstream.WriteLine(" Next")
txtstream.WriteLine("div")
txtstream.WriteLine("")
txtstream.WriteLine("    COLOR: white;")
txtstream.WriteLine("    BACKGROUND-COLOR: black;")
txtstream.WriteLine("    FONT-FAMILY: Cambria, serif;")
txtstream.WriteLine("    FONT-SIZE: 10px;")
txtstream.WriteLine("    text-align: left;")
txtstream.WriteLine("    white-Space: nowrap;")
txtstream.WriteLine(" Next")
txtstream.WriteLine("span")
txtstream.WriteLine("")
txtstream.WriteLine("    COLOR: white;")
txtstream.WriteLine("    BACKGROUND-COLOR: black;")
txtstream.WriteLine("    FONT-FAMILY: Cambria, serif;")
txtstream.WriteLine("    FONT-SIZE: 10px;")
txtstream.WriteLine("    text-align: left;")
txtstream.WriteLine("    white-Space: nowrap;")
txtstream.WriteLine("    display:inline-block;")
txtstream.WriteLine("    width: 100%;")
txtstream.WriteLine(" Next")
txtstream.WriteLine("textarea")
txtstream.WriteLine("")
txtstream.WriteLine("    COLOR: white;")
txtstream.WriteLine("    BACKGROUND-COLOR: black;")
txtstream.WriteLine("    FONT-FAMILY: Cambria, serif;")
txtstream.WriteLine("    FONT-SIZE: 10px;")
```

```
txtstream.WriteLine("    text-align: left;")
txtstream.WriteLine("    white-Space: nowrap;")
txtstream.WriteLine("    width: 100%;")
txtstream.WriteLine(" Next")
txtstream.WriteLine("select")
txtstream.WriteLine("")
txtstream.WriteLine("    COLOR: white;")
txtstream.WriteLine("    BACKGROUND-COLOR: black;")
txtstream.WriteLine("    FONT-FAMILY: Cambria, serif;")
txtstream.WriteLine("    FONT-SIZE: 10px;")
txtstream.WriteLine("    text-align: left;")
txtstream.WriteLine("    white-Space: nowrap;")
txtstream.WriteLine("    width: 100%;")
txtstream.WriteLine(" Next")
txtstream.WriteLine("input")
txtstream.WriteLine("")
txtstream.WriteLine("    COLOR: white;")
txtstream.WriteLine("    BACKGROUND-COLOR: black;")
txtstream.WriteLine("    FONT-FAMILY: Cambria, serif;")
txtstream.WriteLine("    FONT-SIZE: 12px;")
txtstream.WriteLine("    text-align: left;")
txtstream.WriteLine("    display:table-cell;")
txtstream.WriteLine("    white-Space: nowrap;")
txtstream.WriteLine(" Next")
txtstream.WriteLine("h1 ")
txtstream.WriteLine("color: antiquewhite;")
txtstream.WriteLine("text-shadow: 1px 1px 1px black;")
txtstream.WriteLine("padding: 3px;")
txtstream.WriteLine("text-align: center;")
txtstream.WriteLine("box-shadow: inSet 2px 2px 5px rgba(0,0,0,0.5), inSet -
2px -2px 5px rgba(255,255,255,0.5);")
txtstream.WriteLine(" Next")
txtstream.WriteLine("</style>")
```

COLORED TEXT

```
txtstream.WriteLine("<style type='text/css'>")
txtstream.WriteLine("th")
txtstream.WriteLine("")
txtstream.WriteLine("    COLOR: darkred;")
txtstream.WriteLine("    BACKGROUND-COLOR: #eeeeee;")
txtstream.WriteLine("    FONT-FAMILY: Cambria, serif;")
txtstream.WriteLine("    FONT-SIZE: 12px;")
txtstream.WriteLine("    text-align: left;")
txtstream.WriteLine("    white-Space: nowrap;")
txtstream.WriteLine(" Next")
txtstream.WriteLine("td")
txtstream.WriteLine("")
txtstream.WriteLine("    COLOR: navy;")
txtstream.WriteLine("    BACKGROUND-COLOR: #eeeeee;")
txtstream.WriteLine("    FONT-FAMILY: Cambria, serif;")
txtstream.WriteLine("    FONT-SIZE: 12px;")
txtstream.WriteLine("    text-align: left;")
txtstream.WriteLine("    white-Space: nowrap;")
txtstream.WriteLine(" Next")
txtstream.WriteLine("div")
txtstream.WriteLine("")
txtstream.WriteLine("    COLOR: white;")
txtstream.WriteLine("    BACKGROUND-COLOR: navy;")
txtstream.WriteLine("    FONT-FAMILY: Cambria, serif;")
txtstream.WriteLine("    FONT-SIZE: 10px;")
txtstream.WriteLine("    text-align: left;")
txtstream.WriteLine("    white-Space: nowrap;")
txtstream.WriteLine(" Next")
txtstream.WriteLine("span")
txtstream.WriteLine("")
```

```
txtstream.WriteLine("    COLOR: white;")
txtstream.WriteLine("    BACKGROUND-COLOR: navy;")
txtstream.WriteLine("    FONT-FAMILY: Cambria, serif;")
txtstream.WriteLine("    FONT-SIZE: 10px;")
txtstream.WriteLine("    text-align: left;")
txtstream.WriteLine("    white-Space: nowrap;")
txtstream.WriteLine("    display:inline-block;")
txtstream.WriteLine("    width: 100%;")
txtstream.WriteLine(" Next")
txtstream.WriteLine("textarea")
txtstream.WriteLine("")
txtstream.WriteLine("    COLOR: white;")
txtstream.WriteLine("    BACKGROUND-COLOR: navy;")
txtstream.WriteLine("    FONT-FAMILY: Cambria, serif;")
txtstream.WriteLine("    FONT-SIZE: 10px;")
txtstream.WriteLine("    text-align: left;")
txtstream.WriteLine("    white-Space: nowrap;")
txtstream.WriteLine("    width: 100%;")
txtstream.WriteLine(" Next")
txtstream.WriteLine("select")
txtstream.WriteLine("")
txtstream.WriteLine("    COLOR: white;")
txtstream.WriteLine("    BACKGROUND-COLOR: navy;")
txtstream.WriteLine("    FONT-FAMILY: Cambria, serif;")
txtstream.WriteLine("    FONT-SIZE: 10px;")
txtstream.WriteLine("    text-align: left;")
txtstream.WriteLine("    white-Space: nowrap;")
txtstream.WriteLine("    width: 100%;")
txtstream.WriteLine(" Next")
txtstream.WriteLine("input")
txtstream.WriteLine("")
txtstream.WriteLine("    COLOR: white;")
txtstream.WriteLine("    BACKGROUND-COLOR: navy;")
```

```
txtstream.WriteLine("    FONT-FAMILY: Cambria, serif;")
txtstream.WriteLine("    FONT-SIZE: 12px;")
txtstream.WriteLine("    text-align: left;")
txtstream.WriteLine("    display:table-cell;")
txtstream.WriteLine("    white-Space: nowrap;")
txtstream.WriteLine(" Next")
txtstream.WriteLine("h1 ")
txtstream.WriteLine("color: antiquewhite;")
txtstream.WriteLine("text-shadow: 1px 1px 1px black;")
txtstream.WriteLine("padding: 3px;")
txtstream.WriteLine("text-align: center;")
txtstream.WriteLine("box-shadow: inSet 2px 2px 5px rgba(0,0,0,0.5), inSet -2px -2px 5px rgba(255,255,255,0.5);")
txtstream.WriteLine(" Next")
txtstream.WriteLine("</style>")
```

OSCILLATING ROW COLORS

```
txtstream.WriteLine("<style>")
txtstream.WriteLine("th")
txtstream.WriteLine("")
txtstream.WriteLine("    COLOR: white;")
txtstream.WriteLine("    BACKGROUND-COLOR: navy;")
txtstream.WriteLine("    FONT-FAMILY: Cambria, serif;")
txtstream.WriteLine("    FONT-SIZE: 12px;")
txtstream.WriteLine("    text-align: left;")
txtstream.WriteLine("    white-Space: nowrap;")
txtstream.WriteLine(" Next")
txtstream.WriteLine("td")
txtstream.WriteLine("")
txtstream.WriteLine("    COLOR: navy;")
```

txtstream.WriteLine("   FONT-FAMILY: Cambria, serif;")
txtstream.WriteLine("   FONT-SIZE: 12px;")
txtstream.WriteLine("   text-align: left;")
txtstream.WriteLine("   white-Space: nowrap;")
txtstream.WriteLine(" Next")
txtstream.WriteLine("div")
txtstream.WriteLine("")
txtstream.WriteLine("   COLOR: navy;")
txtstream.WriteLine("   FONT-FAMILY: Cambria, serif;")
txtstream.WriteLine("   FONT-SIZE: 12px;")
txtstream.WriteLine("   text-align: left;")
txtstream.WriteLine("   white-Space: nowrap;")
txtstream.WriteLine(" Next")
txtstream.WriteLine("span")
txtstream.WriteLine("")
txtstream.WriteLine("   COLOR: navy;")
txtstream.WriteLine("   FONT-FAMILY: Cambria, serif;")
txtstream.WriteLine("   FONT-SIZE: 12px;")
txtstream.WriteLine("   text-align: left;")
txtstream.WriteLine("   white-Space: nowrap;")
txtstream.WriteLine("   width: 100%;")
txtstream.WriteLine(" Next")
txtstream.WriteLine("textarea")
txtstream.WriteLine("")
txtstream.WriteLine("   COLOR: navy;")
txtstream.WriteLine("   FONT-FAMILY: Cambria, serif;")
txtstream.WriteLine("   FONT-SIZE: 12px;")
txtstream.WriteLine("   text-align: left;")
txtstream.WriteLine("   white-Space: nowrap;")
txtstream.WriteLine("   display:inline-block;")
txtstream.WriteLine("   width: 100%;")
txtstream.WriteLine(" Next")
txtstream.WriteLine("select")

txtstream.WriteLine("")

txtstream.WriteLine("   COLOR: navy;")

txtstream.WriteLine("   FONT-FAMILY: Cambria, serif;")

txtstream.WriteLine("   FONT-SIZE: 10px;")

txtstream.WriteLine("   text-align: left;")

txtstream.WriteLine("   white-Space: nowrap;")

txtstream.WriteLine("   display:inline-block;")

txtstream.WriteLine("   width: 100%;")

txtstream.WriteLine(" Next")

txtstream.WriteLine("input")

txtstream.WriteLine("")

txtstream.WriteLine("   COLOR: navy;")

txtstream.WriteLine("   FONT-FAMILY: Cambria, serif;")

txtstream.WriteLine("   FONT-SIZE: 12px;")

txtstream.WriteLine("   text-align: left;")

txtstream.WriteLine("   display:table-cell;")

txtstream.WriteLine("   white-Space: nowrap;")

txtstream.WriteLine(" Next")

txtstream.WriteLine("h1 ")

txtstream.WriteLine("color: antiquewhite;")

txtstream.WriteLine("text-shadow: 1px 1px 1px black;")

txtstream.WriteLine("padding: 3px;")

txtstream.WriteLine("text-align: center;")

txtstream.WriteLine("box-shadow: inSet 2px 2px 5px rgba(0,0,0,0.5), inSet -2px -2px 5px rgba(255,255,255,0.5);")

txtstream.WriteLine(" Next")

txtstream.WriteLine("tr:nth-child(even)background-color:#f2f2f2; Next")

txtstream.WriteLine("tr:nth-child(odd)background-color:#cccccc; color:#f2f2f2; Next")

txtstream.WriteLine("</style>")

GHOST DECORATED

```
txtstream.WriteLine("<style type='text/css'>")
txtstream.WriteLine("th")
txtstream.WriteLine("")
txtstream.WriteLine("   COLOR: black;")
txtstream.WriteLine("   BACKGROUND-COLOR: white;")
txtstream.WriteLine("   FONT-FAMILY: Cambria, serif;")
txtstream.WriteLine("   FONT-SIZE: 12px;")
txtstream.WriteLine("   text-align: left;")
txtstream.WriteLine("   white-Space: nowrap;")
txtstream.WriteLine(" Next")
txtstream.WriteLine("td")
txtstream.WriteLine("")
txtstream.WriteLine("   COLOR: black;")
txtstream.WriteLine("   BACKGROUND-COLOR: white;")
txtstream.WriteLine("   FONT-FAMILY: Cambria, serif;")
txtstream.WriteLine("   FONT-SIZE: 12px;")
txtstream.WriteLine("   text-align: left;")
txtstream.WriteLine("   white-Space: nowrap;")
txtstream.WriteLine(" Next")
txtstream.WriteLine("div")
txtstream.WriteLine("")
txtstream.WriteLine("   COLOR: black;")
txtstream.WriteLine("   BACKGROUND-COLOR: white;")
txtstream.WriteLine("   FONT-FAMILY: Cambria, serif;")
txtstream.WriteLine("   FONT-SIZE: 10px;")
txtstream.WriteLine("   text-align: left;")
txtstream.WriteLine("   white-Space: nowrap;")
txtstream.WriteLine(" Next")
txtstream.WriteLine("span")
txtstream.WriteLine("")
txtstream.WriteLine("   COLOR: black;")
txtstream.WriteLine("   BACKGROUND-COLOR: white;")
txtstream.WriteLine("   FONT-FAMILY: Cambria, serif;")
```

```
txtstream.WriteLine("    FONT-SIZE: 10px;")
txtstream.WriteLine("    text-align: left;")
txtstream.WriteLine("    white-Space: nowrap;")
txtstream.WriteLine("    display:inline-block;")
txtstream.WriteLine("    width: 100%;")
txtstream.WriteLine(" Next")
txtstream.WriteLine("textarea")
txtstream.WriteLine("")
txtstream.WriteLine("    COLOR: black;")
txtstream.WriteLine("    BACKGROUND-COLOR: white;")
txtstream.WriteLine("    FONT-FAMILY: Cambria, serif;")
txtstream.WriteLine("    FONT-SIZE: 10px;")
txtstream.WriteLine("    text-align: left;")
txtstream.WriteLine("    white-Space: nowrap;")
txtstream.WriteLine("    width: 100%;")
txtstream.WriteLine(" Next")
txtstream.WriteLine("select")
txtstream.WriteLine("")
txtstream.WriteLine("    COLOR: black;")
txtstream.WriteLine("    BACKGROUND-COLOR: white;")
txtstream.WriteLine("    FONT-FAMILY: Cambria, serif;")
txtstream.WriteLine("    FONT-SIZE: 10px;")
txtstream.WriteLine("    text-align: left;")
txtstream.WriteLine("    white-Space: nowrap;")
txtstream.WriteLine("    width: 100%;")
txtstream.WriteLine(" Next")
txtstream.WriteLine("input")
txtstream.WriteLine("")
txtstream.WriteLine("    COLOR: black;")
txtstream.WriteLine("    BACKGROUND-COLOR: white;")
txtstream.WriteLine("    FONT-FAMILY: Cambria, serif;")
txtstream.WriteLine("    FONT-SIZE: 12px;")
txtstream.WriteLine("    text-align: left;")
```

```
txtstream.WriteLine("    display:table-cell;")
txtstream.WriteLine("    white-Space: nowrap;")
txtstream.WriteLine(" Next")
txtstream.WriteLine("h1 ")
txtstream.WriteLine("color: antiquewhite;")
txtstream.WriteLine("text-shadow: 1px 1px 1px black;")
txtstream.WriteLine("padding: 3px;")
txtstream.WriteLine("text-align: center;")
txtstream.WriteLine("box-shadow: inSet 2px 2px 5px rgba(0,0,0,0.5), inSet -2px -2px 5px rgba(255,255,255,0.5);")
txtstream.WriteLine(" Next")
txtstream.WriteLine("</style>")
```

3D

```
txtstream.WriteLine("<style type='text/css'>")
txtstream.WriteLine("body")
txtstream.WriteLine("")
txtstream.WriteLine("    PADDING-RIGHT: 0px;")
txtstream.WriteLine("    PADDING-LEFT: 0px;")
txtstream.WriteLine("    PADDING-BOTTOM: 0px;")
txtstream.WriteLine("    MARGIN: 0px;")
txtstream.WriteLine("    COLOR: #333;")
txtstream.WriteLine("    PADDING-TOP: 0px;")
txtstream.WriteLine("    FONT-FAMILY: verdana, arial, helvetica, sans-serif;")
txtstream.WriteLine(" Next")
txtstream.WriteLine("table")
txtstream.WriteLine("")
txtstream.WriteLine("    BORDER-RIGHT: #999999 3px solid;")
txtstream.WriteLine("    PADDING-RIGHT: 6px;")
txtstream.WriteLine("    PADDING-LEFT: 6px;")
txtstream.WriteLine("    FONT-WEIGHT: Bold;")
```

```
txtstream.WriteLine("    FONT-SIZE: 14px;")
txtstream.WriteLine("    PADDING-BOTTOM: 6px;")
txtstream.WriteLine("    COLOR: Peru;")
txtstream.WriteLine("    LINE-HEIGHT: 14px;")
txtstream.WriteLine("    PADDING-TOP: 6px;")
txtstream.WriteLine("    BORDER-BOTTOM: #999 1px solid;")
txtstream.WriteLine("    BACKGROUND-COLOR: #eeeeee;")
txtstream.WriteLine("    FONT-FAMILY: verdana, arial, helvetica, sans-serif;")
txtstream.WriteLine("    FONT-SIZE: 12px;")
txtstream.WriteLine(" Next")
txtstream.WriteLine("th")
txtstream.WriteLine("")
txtstream.WriteLine("    BORDER-RIGHT: #999999 3px solid;")
txtstream.WriteLine("    PADDING-RIGHT: 6px;")
txtstream.WriteLine("    PADDING-LEFT: 6px;")
txtstream.WriteLine("    FONT-WEIGHT: Bold;")
txtstream.WriteLine("    FONT-SIZE: 14px;")
txtstream.WriteLine("    PADDING-BOTTOM: 6px;")
txtstream.WriteLine("    COLOR: darkred;")
txtstream.WriteLine("    LINE-HEIGHT: 14px;")
txtstream.WriteLine("    PADDING-TOP: 6px;")
txtstream.WriteLine("    BORDER-BOTTOM: #999 1px solid;")
txtstream.WriteLine("    BACKGROUND-COLOR: #eeeeee;")
txtstream.WriteLine("    FONT-FAMILY: Cambria, serif;")
txtstream.WriteLine("    FONT-SIZE: 12px;")
txtstream.WriteLine("    text-align: left;")
txtstream.WriteLine("    white-Space: nowrap;")
txtstream.WriteLine(" Next")
txtstream.WriteLine(".th")
txtstream.WriteLine("")
txtstream.WriteLine("    BORDER-RIGHT: #999999 2px solid;")
txtstream.WriteLine("    PADDING-RIGHT: 6px;")
txtstream.WriteLine("    PADDING-LEFT: 6px;")
```

txtstream.WriteLine("   FONT-WEIGHT: Bold;")

txtstream.WriteLine("   PADDING-BOTTOM: 6px;")

txtstream.WriteLine("   COLOR: black;")

txtstream.WriteLine("   PADDING-TOP: 6px;")

txtstream.WriteLine("   BORDER-BOTTOM: #999 2px solid;")

txtstream.WriteLine("   BACKGROUND-COLOR: #eeeeee;")

txtstream.WriteLine("   FONT-FAMILY: Cambria, serif;")

txtstream.WriteLine("   FONT-SIZE: 10px;")

txtstream.WriteLine("   text-align: right;")

txtstream.WriteLine("   white-Space: nowrap;")

txtstream.WriteLine(" Next")

txtstream.WriteLine("td")

txtstream.WriteLine("")

txtstream.WriteLine("   BORDER-RIGHT: #999999 3px solid;")

txtstream.WriteLine("   PADDING-RIGHT: 6px;")

txtstream.WriteLine("   PADDING-LEFT: 6px;")

txtstream.WriteLine("   FONT-WEIGHT: Normal;")

txtstream.WriteLine("   PADDING-BOTTOM: 6px;")

txtstream.WriteLine("   COLOR: navy;")

txtstream.WriteLine("   LINE-HEIGHT: 14px;")

txtstream.WriteLine("   PADDING-TOP: 6px;")

txtstream.WriteLine("   BORDER-BOTTOM: #999 1px solid;")

txtstream.WriteLine("   BACKGROUND-COLOR: #eeeeee;")

txtstream.WriteLine("   FONT-FAMILY: Cambria, serif;")

txtstream.WriteLine("   FONT-SIZE: 12px;")

txtstream.WriteLine("   text-align: left;")

txtstream.WriteLine("   white-Space: nowrap;")

txtstream.WriteLine(" Next")

txtstream.WriteLine("div")

txtstream.WriteLine("")

txtstream.WriteLine("   BORDER-RIGHT: #999999 3px solid;")

txtstream.WriteLine("   PADDING-RIGHT: 6px;")

txtstream.WriteLine("   PADDING-LEFT: 6px;")

```
txtstream.WriteLine("   FONT-WEIGHT: Normal;")
txtstream.WriteLine("   PADDING-BOTTOM: 6px;")
txtstream.WriteLine("   COLOR: white;")
txtstream.WriteLine("   PADDING-TOP: 6px;")
txtstream.WriteLine("   BORDER-BOTTOM: #999 1px solid;")
txtstream.WriteLine("   BACKGROUND-COLOR: navy;")
txtstream.WriteLine("   FONT-FAMILY: Cambria, serif;")
txtstream.WriteLine("   FONT-SIZE: 10px;")
txtstream.WriteLine("   text-align: left;")
txtstream.WriteLine("   white-Space: nowrap;")
txtstream.WriteLine(" Next")
txtstream.WriteLine("span")
txtstream.WriteLine("")
txtstream.WriteLine("   BORDER-RIGHT: #999999 3px solid;")
txtstream.WriteLine("   PADDING-RIGHT: 3px;")
txtstream.WriteLine("   PADDING-LEFT: 3px;")
txtstream.WriteLine("   FONT-WEIGHT: Normal;")
txtstream.WriteLine("   PADDING-BOTTOM: 3px;")
txtstream.WriteLine("   COLOR: white;")
txtstream.WriteLine("   PADDING-TOP: 3px;")
txtstream.WriteLine("   BORDER-BOTTOM: #999 1px solid;")
txtstream.WriteLine("   BACKGROUND-COLOR: navy;")
txtstream.WriteLine("   FONT-FAMILY: Cambria, serif;")
txtstream.WriteLine("   FONT-SIZE: 10px;")
txtstream.WriteLine("   text-align: left;")
txtstream.WriteLine("   white-Space: nowrap;")
txtstream.WriteLine("   display:inline-block;")
txtstream.WriteLine("   width: 100%;")
txtstream.WriteLine(" Next")
txtstream.WriteLine("textarea")
txtstream.WriteLine("")
txtstream.WriteLine("   BORDER-RIGHT: #999999 3px solid;")
txtstream.WriteLine("   PADDING-RIGHT: 3px;")
```

```
txtstream.WriteLine("    PADDING-LEFT: 3px;")
txtstream.WriteLine("    FONT-WEIGHT: Normal;")
txtstream.WriteLine("    PADDING-BOTTOM: 3px;")
txtstream.WriteLine("    COLOR: white;")
txtstream.WriteLine("    PADDING-TOP: 3px;")
txtstream.WriteLine("    BORDER-BOTTOM: #999 1px solid;")
txtstream.WriteLine("    BACKGROUND-COLOR: navy;")
txtstream.WriteLine("    FONT-FAMILY: Cambria, serif;")
txtstream.WriteLine("    FONT-SIZE: 10px;")
txtstream.WriteLine("    text-align: left;")
txtstream.WriteLine("    white-Space: nowrap;")
txtstream.WriteLine("    width: 100%;")
txtstream.WriteLine(" Next")
txtstream.WriteLine("select")
txtstream.WriteLine("")
txtstream.WriteLine("    BORDER-RIGHT: #999999 3px solid;")
txtstream.WriteLine("    PADDING-RIGHT: 6px;")
txtstream.WriteLine("    PADDING-LEFT: 6px;")
txtstream.WriteLine("    FONT-WEIGHT: Normal;")
txtstream.WriteLine("    PADDING-BOTTOM: 6px;")
txtstream.WriteLine("    COLOR: white;")
txtstream.WriteLine("    PADDING-TOP: 6px;")
txtstream.WriteLine("    BORDER-BOTTOM: #999 1px solid;")
txtstream.WriteLine("    BACKGROUND-COLOR: navy;")
txtstream.WriteLine("    FONT-FAMILY: Cambria, serif;")
txtstream.WriteLine("    FONT-SIZE: 10px;")
txtstream.WriteLine("    text-align: left;")
txtstream.WriteLine("    white-Space: nowrap;")
txtstream.WriteLine("    width: 100%;")
txtstream.WriteLine(" Next")
txtstream.WriteLine("input")
txtstream.WriteLine("")
txtstream.WriteLine("    BORDER-RIGHT: #999999 3px solid;")
```

```
txtstream.WriteLine("    PADDING-RIGHT: 3px;")
txtstream.WriteLine("    PADDING-LEFT: 3px;")
txtstream.WriteLine("    FONT-WEIGHT: Bold;")
txtstream.WriteLine("    PADDING-BOTTOM: 3px;")
txtstream.WriteLine("    COLOR: white;")
txtstream.WriteLine("    PADDING-TOP: 3px;")
txtstream.WriteLine("    BORDER-BOTTOM: #999 1px solid;")
txtstream.WriteLine("    BACKGROUND-COLOR: navy;")
txtstream.WriteLine("    FONT-FAMILY: Cambria, serif;")
txtstream.WriteLine("    FONT-SIZE: 12px;")
txtstream.WriteLine("    text-align: left;")
txtstream.WriteLine("    display:table-cell;")
txtstream.WriteLine("    white-Space: nowrap;")
txtstream.WriteLine("    width: 100%;")
txtstream.WriteLine(" Next")
txtstream.WriteLine("h1 ")
txtstream.WriteLine("color: antiquewhite;")
txtstream.WriteLine("text-shadow: 1px 1px 1px black;")
txtstream.WriteLine("padding: 3px;")
txtstream.WriteLine("text-align: center;")
txtstream.WriteLine("box-shadow: inSet 2px 2px 5px rgba(0,0,0,0.5), inSet -
2px -2px 5px rgba(255,255,255,0.5);")
txtstream.WriteLine(" Next")
txtstream.WriteLine("</style>")
```

SHADOW BOX

```
txtstream.WriteLine("<style type='text/css'>")
txtstream.WriteLine("body")
txtstream.WriteLine("")
txtstream.WriteLine("    PADDING-RIGHT: 0px;")
txtstream.WriteLine("    PADDING-LEFT: 0px;")
txtstream.WriteLine("    PADDING-BOTTOM: 0px;")
```

```
txtstream.WriteLine("    MARGIN: 0px;")
txtstream.WriteLine("    COLOR: #333;")
txtstream.WriteLine("    PADDING-TOP: 0px;")
txtstream.WriteLine("    FONT-FAMILY: verdana, arial, helvetica, sans-serif;")
txtstream.WriteLine(" Next")
txtstream.WriteLine("table")
txtstream.WriteLine("")
txtstream.WriteLine("    BORDER-RIGHT: #999999 1px solid;")
txtstream.WriteLine("    PADDING-RIGHT: 1px;")
txtstream.WriteLine("    PADDING-LEFT: 1px;")
txtstream.WriteLine("    PADDING-BOTTOM: 1px;")
txtstream.WriteLine("    LINE-HEIGHT: 8px;")
txtstream.WriteLine("    PADDING-TOP: 1px;")
txtstream.WriteLine("    BORDER-BOTTOM: #999 1px solid;")
txtstream.WriteLine("    BACKGROUND-COLOR: #eeeeee;")
txtstream.WriteLine("
filter:progid:DXImageTransform.Microsoft.Shadow(color='silver',    Direction=135,
Strength=16)")
txtstream.WriteLine(" Next")
txtstream.WriteLine("th")
txtstream.WriteLine("")
txtstream.WriteLine("    BORDER-RIGHT: #999999 3px solid;")
txtstream.WriteLine("    PADDING-RIGHT: 6px;")
txtstream.WriteLine("    PADDING-LEFT: 6px;")
txtstream.WriteLine("    FONT-WEIGHT: Bold;")
txtstream.WriteLine("    FONT-SIZE: 14px;")
txtstream.WriteLine("    PADDING-BOTTOM: 6px;")
txtstream.WriteLine("    COLOR: darkred;")
txtstream.WriteLine("    LINE-HEIGHT: 14px;")
txtstream.WriteLine("    PADDING-TOP: 6px;")
txtstream.WriteLine("    BORDER-BOTTOM: #999 1px solid;")
txtstream.WriteLine("    BACKGROUND-COLOR: #eeeeee;")
txtstream.WriteLine("    FONT-FAMILY: Cambria, serif;")
```

```
txtstream.WriteLine("   FONT-SIZE: 12px;")
txtstream.WriteLine("   text-align: left;")
txtstream.WriteLine("   white-Space: nowrap;")
txtstream.WriteLine(" Next")
txtstream.WriteLine(".th")
txtstream.WriteLine("")
txtstream.WriteLine("   BORDER-RIGHT: #999999 2px solid;")
txtstream.WriteLine("   PADDING-RIGHT: 6px;")
txtstream.WriteLine("   PADDING-LEFT: 6px;")
txtstream.WriteLine("   FONT-WEIGHT: Bold;")
txtstream.WriteLine("   PADDING-BOTTOM: 6px;")
txtstream.WriteLine("   COLOR: black;")
txtstream.WriteLine("   PADDING-TOP: 6px;")
txtstream.WriteLine("   BORDER-BOTTOM: #999 2px solid;")
txtstream.WriteLine("   BACKGROUND-COLOR: #eeeeee;")
txtstream.WriteLine("   FONT-FAMILY: Cambria, serif;")
txtstream.WriteLine("   FONT-SIZE: 10px;")
txtstream.WriteLine("   text-align: right;")
txtstream.WriteLine("   white-Space: nowrap;")
txtstream.WriteLine(" Next")
txtstream.WriteLine("td")
txtstream.WriteLine("")
txtstream.WriteLine("   BORDER-RIGHT: #999999 3px solid;")
txtstream.WriteLine("   PADDING-RIGHT: 6px;")
txtstream.WriteLine("   PADDING-LEFT: 6px;")
txtstream.WriteLine("   FONT-WEIGHT: Normal;")
txtstream.WriteLine("   PADDING-BOTTOM: 6px;")
txtstream.WriteLine("   COLOR: navy;")
txtstream.WriteLine("   LINE-HEIGHT: 14px;")
txtstream.WriteLine("   PADDING-TOP: 6px;")
txtstream.WriteLine("   BORDER-BOTTOM: #999 1px solid;")
txtstream.WriteLine("   BACKGROUND-COLOR: #eeeeee;")
txtstream.WriteLine("   FONT-FAMILY: Cambria, serif;")
```

txtstream.WriteLine("   FONT-SIZE: 12px;")

txtstream.WriteLine("   text-align: left;")

txtstream.WriteLine("   white-Space: nowrap;")

txtstream.WriteLine(" Next")

txtstream.WriteLine("div")

txtstream.WriteLine("")

txtstream.WriteLine("   BORDER-RIGHT: #999999 3px solid;")

txtstream.WriteLine("   PADDING-RIGHT: 6px;")

txtstream.WriteLine("   PADDING-LEFT: 6px;")

txtstream.WriteLine("   FONT-WEIGHT: Normal;")

txtstream.WriteLine("   PADDING-BOTTOM: 6px;")

txtstream.WriteLine("   COLOR: white;")

txtstream.WriteLine("   PADDING-TOP: 6px;")

txtstream.WriteLine("   BORDER-BOTTOM: #999 1px solid;")

txtstream.WriteLine("   BACKGROUND-COLOR: navy;")

txtstream.WriteLine("   FONT-FAMILY: Cambria, serif;")

txtstream.WriteLine("   FONT-SIZE: 10px;")

txtstream.WriteLine("   text-align: left;")

txtstream.WriteLine("   white-Space: nowrap;")

txtstream.WriteLine(" Next")

txtstream.WriteLine("span")

txtstream.WriteLine("")

txtstream.WriteLine("   BORDER-RIGHT: #999999 3px solid;")

txtstream.WriteLine("   PADDING-RIGHT: 3px;")

txtstream.WriteLine("   PADDING-LEFT: 3px;")

txtstream.WriteLine("   FONT-WEIGHT: Normal;")

txtstream.WriteLine("   PADDING-BOTTOM: 3px;")

txtstream.WriteLine("   COLOR: white;")

txtstream.WriteLine("   PADDING-TOP: 3px;")

txtstream.WriteLine("   BORDER-BOTTOM: #999 1px solid;")

txtstream.WriteLine("   BACKGROUND-COLOR: navy;")

txtstream.WriteLine("   FONT-FAMILY: Cambria, serif;")

txtstream.WriteLine("   FONT-SIZE: 10px;")

```
txtstream.WriteLine("    text-align: left;")
txtstream.WriteLine("    white-Space: nowrap;")
txtstream.WriteLine("    display: inline-block;")
txtstream.WriteLine("    width: 100%;")
txtstream.WriteLine(" Next")
txtstream.WriteLine("textarea")
txtstream.WriteLine("")
txtstream.WriteLine("    BORDER-RIGHT: #999999 3px solid;")
txtstream.WriteLine("    PADDING-RIGHT: 3px;")
txtstream.WriteLine("    PADDING-LEFT: 3px;")
txtstream.WriteLine("    FONT-WEIGHT: Normal;")
txtstream.WriteLine("    PADDING-BOTTOM: 3px;")
txtstream.WriteLine("    COLOR: white;")
txtstream.WriteLine("    PADDING-TOP: 3px;")
txtstream.WriteLine("    BORDER-BOTTOM: #999 1px solid;")
txtstream.WriteLine("    BACKGROUND-COLOR: navy;")
txtstream.WriteLine("    FONT-FAMILY: Cambria, serif;")
txtstream.WriteLine("    FONT-SIZE: 10px;")
txtstream.WriteLine("    text-align: left;")
txtstream.WriteLine("    white-Space: nowrap;")
txtstream.WriteLine("    width: 100%;")
txtstream.WriteLine(" Next")
txtstream.WriteLine("select")
txtstream.WriteLine("")
txtstream.WriteLine("    BORDER-RIGHT: #999999 3px solid;")
txtstream.WriteLine("    PADDING-RIGHT: 6px;")
txtstream.WriteLine("    PADDING-LEFT: 6px;")
txtstream.WriteLine("    FONT-WEIGHT: Normal;")
txtstream.WriteLine("    PADDING-BOTTOM: 6px;")
txtstream.WriteLine("    COLOR: white;")
txtstream.WriteLine("    PADDING-TOP: 6px;")
txtstream.WriteLine("    BORDER-BOTTOM: #999 1px solid;")
txtstream.WriteLine("    BACKGROUND-COLOR: navy;")
```

```
txtstream.WriteLine("   FONT-FAMILY: Cambria, serif;")
txtstream.WriteLine("   FONT-SIZE: 10px;")
txtstream.WriteLine("   text-align: left;")
txtstream.WriteLine("   white-Space: nowrap;")
txtstream.WriteLine("   width: 100%;")
txtstream.WriteLine(" Next")
txtstream.WriteLine("input")
txtstream.WriteLine(""")
txtstream.WriteLine("   BORDER-RIGHT: #999999 3px solid;")
txtstream.WriteLine("   PADDING-RIGHT: 3px;")
txtstream.WriteLine("   PADDING-LEFT: 3px;")
txtstream.WriteLine("   FONT-WEIGHT: Bold;")
txtstream.WriteLine("   PADDING-BOTTOM: 3px;")
txtstream.WriteLine("   COLOR: white;")
txtstream.WriteLine("   PADDING-TOP: 3px;")
txtstream.WriteLine("   BORDER-BOTTOM: #999 1px solid;")
txtstream.WriteLine("   BACKGROUND-COLOR: navy;")
txtstream.WriteLine("   FONT-FAMILY: Cambria, serif;")
txtstream.WriteLine("   FONT-SIZE: 12px;")
txtstream.WriteLine("   text-align: left;")
txtstream.WriteLine("   display: table-cell;")
txtstream.WriteLine("   white-Space: nowrap;")
txtstream.WriteLine("   width: 100%;")
txtstream.WriteLine(" Next")
txtstream.WriteLine("h1 ")
txtstream.WriteLine("color: antiquewhite;")
txtstream.WriteLine("text-shadow: 1px 1px 1px black;")
txtstream.WriteLine("padding: 3px;")
txtstream.WriteLine("text-align: center;")
txtstream.WriteLine("box-shadow: inSet 2px 2px 5px rgba(0,0,0,0.5), inSet -2px -2px 5px rgba(255,255,255,0.5);")
txtstream.WriteLine(" Next")
txtstream.WriteLine("</style>")
```

Who said you could drop out

What! You can't Drop out! This is an e-book!

How can you drop out of a class if you aren't in one, right?

My first experience of a student wanting to drop out of a college class was based on a heated conversation between the professor and the student. I'm not quite certain why the student felt the way she did considering the professor was an excellent, well known poet.

But for some reason only known to her, she didn't take much liking to him and she wasn't in his class past that point.

Which brings me to my real point that I want to make in your behalf. I don't have to be liked by you. Nor do you have to return the favor. The bottom line here is you are investing the use of your time, effort and money into this book because it is going to gratify your interest of wanting to learn a programming language.

One that, in return is going to make you look smarter on paper, increase your wages and otherwise help you become the superman or superwoman.

Well, I can't promise that. At least, not all of that.

You are paying me to share with you my 30 years-worth of time in front of a computer screen in hopes some of that genie stuff will wear off on you. I can't promise that either. Yes, I am well familiar with the fact that this is the chapter where you decide to purchase this e-book. But, I don't want to motivate you if you're just looking for page after page of code.

You can get that from the internet for free. Instead, I'm taking a more relaxed approach and hope you will appreciate the fact that I know learning a computer language is more than knowing what is needed to code with it. You have to sell yourself and your skills to others. After all, if you can't do that, I don't care how popular the language here is in helping you land a job, not helping you own the right to respectful wages is actually more important.

Otherwise, nothing changes in your life no matter how passionate you are about becoming a freelance programmer or IT consultant. Still want to close the introduction to this book and walk away?

Great!

I don't have to worry about you being my competition the next time I go in for an int

www.ingramcontent.com/pod-product-compliance
Lightning Source LLC
LaVergne TN
LVHW051746050326
832903LV00029B/2748